CRUSH IT ON LINKEDin

BUILD YOUR BRAND GET HIRED & EXPAND YOUR BUSINESS

ISHAN SHARMA

Contents

About the Author   5

Introduction   7

What to do on LinkedIn   10

LinkedIn Connections   13

LinkedIn Content   17

LinkedIn Profile   41

LinkedIn Messaging   66

Grow your Presence on Li   69

LinkedIn Jobs   71

LinkedIn Advertising   75

Don'ts on LinkedIn	**80**
Success Story of Lewis Howes	**84**
LinkedIn Stories	**87**
Use it or Lose it!	**90**

About the Author

I am Ishan Sharma, a 19 year old, second year student from BITS Goa, studying Electrical Engineering. I also own a podcast and YouTube channel where I talk about software development, social media, and entrepreneurship.

You might imagine, how will a 19 year old college student tell me how to build my brand, get a job, or expand my business.

I would think the same way, but the reason is, I have tried most of what you'll read in the book! I have gotten internship and speaking opportunities through LinkedIn, built somewhat of a "brand" in my niche, and have also helped businesses realise how they can leverage social media, and LinkedIn more specifically, to get more leads and customers.

I've done all this in the past one year, and in this book, I'll share with you the tips, tools and strategies that will enable you to achieve your career goals using the power of LinkedIn and networking.

So, if you are ready to unlock the power of LinkedIn and learn some new skills, make sure you click a photo of the book, and tag me on the following social media:

LinkedIn: Ishan Sharma
Twitter: @Ishan739
Instagram: @ishansharma7390

Special Thanks to Visthruth G for designing the cover of this book. And to my parents Pankaj Sharma and Bhawana Sharma for constantly motivating me to write the book and get it out ASAP! Without these amazing people, this book wouldn't have been released in July.

To the Reader: Thanks for taking your time to read this book. I have my birthday on 13th July and so consider this as my birthday gift to you! You've taken the decision to learn and grow yourself. You are different than most people who crave instant gratification and dopamine hits.

Now, let's jump right in!

INTRODUCTION

Wikipedia says and I quote, "LinkedIn is a business and employment oriented online platform that operates as a website and as a downloadable app on iOS and android. Launched on May 5, 2003, LinkedIn is a platform for professionals to connect with each other and create opportunities."

I say LinkedIn is the biggest untapped opportunity of 2020 and this coming decade, a platform to build great connections, find a community full of like-minded people and expand your business.

This book is aimed at people that are in college, or people that work for companies or people that have their own businesses and wish to expand it by finding others that have a similar goal.

This book is framed in 4 parts explaining you, what LinkedIn is, what you can do with it, how other people have leveraged LinkedIn to get jobs, build their brand and business, and lastly, what lies ahead for LinkedIn as a platform.

I am Ishan Sharma, second year student from BITS Goa studying electrical engineering, and I believe that

LinkedIn is the answer for most of you readers trying to build their personal brand, expand your business, and off course get a job and I hope that at the end of reading this book, you'd be convinced with my belief.

Now you may be thinking, how out of all the people in the world, a college student going to tell you how to get this done. What you're thinking is totally reasonable. Most college students never make their LinkedIn profiles until late into their careers.

I, however, made my LinkedIn profile the day my college entrance exam (IIT JEE if you know what that is) got over because I learned from people like Kalpit Veerwal the power of networking and the thought of selling yourself online. I was also reading books like Steve Jobs by Walter Isaacson and How to Win Friends and Influence People by Dale Carnegie, and so I was getting access to these amazing ideas of how people communicate and how the corporate sector works.

So, I started reading what people were talking about on LinkedIn. I started connecting with people who were in college and are into coding and software development. I started interacting and engaging with people through comments and direct messaging.

But, it wasn't until 4 months later, that I started making my own content on the platform, and started engaging with people from all backgrounds. I was always curious about how are these people able to get to the place where they are right now and what were their challenges. That's probably the reason I started my podcast.

Anyways, I started my podcast and made my own YouTube channel and used LinkedIn to leverage my podcast and the YT channel. I started cold messaging some very well-known personalities in my space and learned about what sort of messages get replied back and what my intent should be like while talking to them. I learned what sort of content gets traction on LinkedIn and what content is pure BS and must be avoided if you want to properly use the platform and not get banned.

The following chapters will go in depth over what your LinkedIn profile should look like, what are the different types of content that you can post on LinkedIn, hacks to grow your LinkedIn presence, how to connect with anyone on LinkedIn, how to talk to people on LinkedIn, and lastly, what lies ahead and how the platform will evolve going into this new decade.

My hope by the end of reading this book is that you'll recognize why LinkedIn is the most underrated platform and would be able to create content on LinkedIn that will be engaging and basically CRUSH IT on LinkedIn!

What to do on LinkedIn?

What is Your WHY?

This would be important to ask yourself first before you do just about anything in life. I really like what Simon Sinek says in his book, "Start With WHY" about finding your purpose first and then thinking about the "HOW" and the "WHAT". I would encourage you to check out his TED talk for more context into what I mean.

But basically, it's crucial to think and ask yourself what is it that you really want from your life, and be specific about it. Many people reply to this saying, "Oh, I just wanna be happy", no that's too broad! I want you to write it down on a piece of paper and stick it in your room and be focused on that.

You want a job in a particular industry? You want to start your own business? You Want to build a personal brand? Write it down before you proceed further into the book.

Depending on your choice, there would be different options for what you can do on LinkedIn.

Now let's talk about what might be the most important step in your journey to get where you want to be - CONTENT

MAKE! MAKE! MAKE!

This is what a serial entrepreneur, and marketing expert Gary Vaynerchuk replied when he was asked the question, "How should I get new clients for my restaurant business?"

What has happened in the recent 20 years in marketing is the democratization of marketing, anyone can get in front of people around the world. Not too long ago, people used to pay to get their brand in front of people on TV and radio. I don't say it doesn't exist right now, but it's just not the most efficient way. The thought that you can post a video/picture/text on a platform and anyone could potentially watch it was crazy at the least for anyone 20 years ago.

Moreover, you can do this for free, and use organic reach for your content to be discovered by anyone worldwide. This is the power of social media.

Conventionally, you would think about Instagram and Facebook. But unfortunately, these platforms are past their golden days. But there is one that has the highest organic reach for the content you post on it - LinkedIn.

Yes, I agree, it will go away like it did on Instagram and Facebook, but that's the reason why you must take action NOW before it's too long.

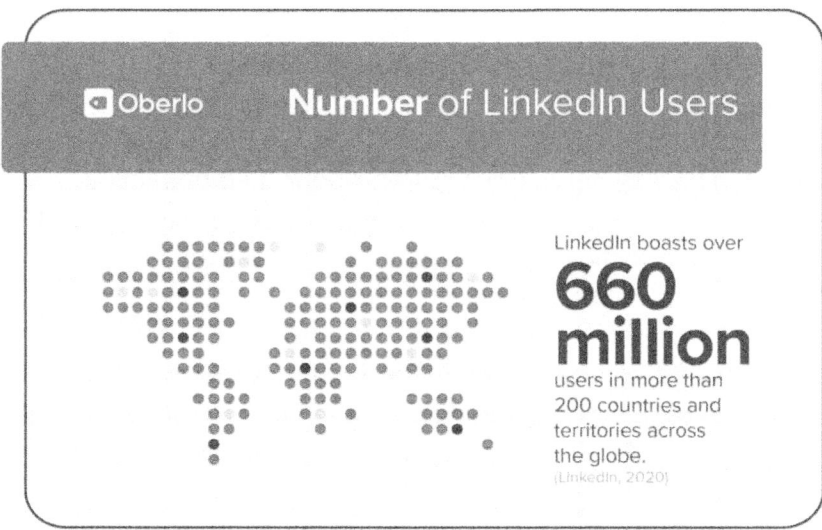

On the date of writing this book, LinkedIn has over 660 Million users using the platform. That number might seem big, but when you look at the amount of people that are creating content on LinkedIn, you understand what I mean.

Only 3 Million out of the 660 Million are people that have posted at least one post on LinkedIn.
Moreover, out of those 3 Million, only 130K post regular content on LinkedIn.

That's a mere 2% of the user base. That means there are less creators and more consumers, leading to more Organic reach for your content.

It's important to note here that not all types of content will get that reach that is mentioned above. But more on that later.
First, let's discuss what connections are and what are best practices when connecting with someone.

Connections

Connecting is like a friend request on Facebook, but more professional.

For you, People will be separated by 4 connection levels: 1st Degree, 2nd Degree, 3rd Degree and 3+ Connection.

The 1st Degree connections are people you have already connected with. These are people closest to you. The 2nd Degree people are the ones who are connected to your 1st degree connections. This is your target audience that you should try to connect with as much as possible.

When your posts are getting engagement within your 1st connections, LinkedIn pushes your post out to 2nd Degree people.

3rd Degree are the people who are connected with your 2nd degree people.

Your target should be to connect with 2nd degree connections the most, so that the people in the 3rd degree group become 2nd degree and so on.

The People who are in the 3rd+ range are generally people who have no connection with your field or industry. You can connect with them if you want to, but

I would recommend you to really focus on connecting with your 2nd degree connections first.

When you send a connection request, you get the option to add a personal message for that person. This increases the likelihood of them accepting your connection. This is something I can tell from my own personal experience.

This does not mean that you'll tell them to sign up for your newsletter or try to be "salesy". That never works and it'll only waste your time and energy.

Some people send a welcome message saying "Hey Ishan, thanks for connecting with me, I hope we'll benefit from each other" or something. You can do this if you want to.

Here are some examples:

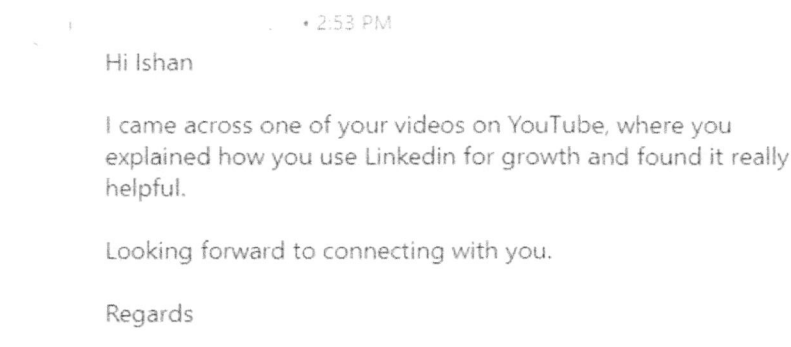

> ⋅ 12:40 PM
>
> Hey Ishan!
> After seeing your profile I couldn't help but send you a connection request! as I literally have so much to learn from you!
> I hope you'll consider connecting.
> stay safe !

Some people on the other hand start selling their products immediately once I accept the connection request. This is another malpractice.

Like this one:

> ⋅ 2:36 PM
>
> Thanks for connecting! Hope you're doing well.
> Its our humble request to support us in our IT company with your valuable like & follow of our page.
> https://www.linkedin.com/company/agumentiksoftware
>
>  Agumentik Software Private Limited | LinkedIn
> linkedin.com

For people in your 3rd degree connection, you can send them an In Mail Message. For a free account you can do this only a few times per month. You can also get the LinkedIn Premium membership to get unlimited In Mail Messages.

Here's an In Mail Message I've sent that the person responded to:

Ishan Sharma • 10:21 AM

Invitation to Podcast

Hello .
I am Ishan, and I have a Podcast called BITS Cast, where I talk about college, life, entrepreneurship and more.

Check it out here : https://linktr.ee/bitscast

Would it be possible for you to join me for an episode, it'll be great to talk to you!
Let me know!!

Once you have 500 connections, the connect button on your profile changes to follow and if you want to connect, you can click on More, to find that option.

Now, let's talk about the different types of content you can make and which ones are better.

LinkedIn Content

Ever wondered what's the answer to building a brand, or getting hired, or building your business? Assuming that what you wanted to know the answer to when picking this book to read, let me help you out!

It's called Content. The single most important word to that question is content.
Another important thing to remember is the context of the content that you're putting out. Posting a selfie of you on a sunny day chilling on the beach might work for your Instagram and Facebook, but not so much for LinkedIn.

Context means understanding who the person on the other side looking at your post is, and how the content you are making is related to them. LinkedIn is not the place for you to post pictures of your cat or dog.

The community on LinkedIn is more inclined towards learning new skills, tips, tricks, opportunities, etc that helps them in some way.

There are multiple ways in which you can create content on the platform, namely:
1. Long Form Posts

2. Pictures
3. PDF Documents
4. Video
5. Article
6. LinkedIn Live

Now, let's discuss these in depth.

Update/Post

The most basic way to make content on LinkedIn is by writing a long form post, which acts sort of like a blogpost. There is a limit of 1300 characters and you can find it on the top of your home feed on the website. There are multiple documents that you can attach to it, like pictures, video, and PDF.

When writing a post, you should know that if it exceeds 140 characters or 3 lines, LinkedIn cuts off the sentence with a "See More" option. Hence, if you want people to engage with your post, make sure it's more than 140 characters and uses empty spaces.

The trick here is to use spaces to your advantage. It's better to write 1-3 lines and leave a line before writing more. It looks less cluttered and more readable. LinkedIn will promote posts that are longer. (this may change anytime)

Also, some of the best performing posts I've seen were about people sharing their personal experiences, and the struggles they've had. It was found out that posts with pictures have a 98% more engagement rate than regular posts.

Like email marketing and YouTube videos, creating hooks can skyrocket your engagement. This, like many other things, is a skill that you'll only learn with experimentation. You can also start off with a question that sparks interest in the mind of the person while scrolling through the feed.

Another thing to remember is the use of hashtags. The way hashtags work on LinkedIn is very different from other platforms like Instagram wherein you would use 30 different sized hashtags in a post to get higher into the explore feed.

Don't do that on LinkedIn, use 5-10 very specific hashtags and that's it. When you release a post, the platform first shows it to your 1st degree connections, and if a lot of people seem to engage with it, then it pushes it to your 2nd degree connections.

One pro tip (for those trying to build a brand on the platform): make your own hashtag. You can basically just come up with some short word that represents you and use that as your very own hashtag, for example #ishan.

People can follow #ishan to see more posts by you and you can see who else is talking about you when they use #ishan on their own post.

Some people also tag themselves and their business at the end of their posts. This way, when the person reading the post reaches the end, they can quickly take a look at who you are and what you do.

So, now you've published your very first post, what's next?

You need people to engage with it early on, and so a little trick I use is to send the link of my post to my friends who like and comment on it, that way LinkedIn pushes it to more people.
If LinkedIn sees that no one has engaged with your post in the first 1 hour, it won't show it to a lot of people.

If you can form a group chat on LinkedIn with all your friends, that can help your posts a lot. Once you complete writing your post, send its link in the group. Other members can click on that link to engage with your post early on, leading to LinkedIn showing it to more people. ANd then you would do the same for other people as well in the group.

These groups are also called Engagement groups. Many people don't like to use it, calling it "fake" engagement, which is true to an extent. At the end, I'll leave it to you to decide to use it or not.

Another metric that governs how your post performs, is the time of the day you release it. A lot of people are active in evenings and night time on the platform and so it makes more sense to release it around that time.

Recipe for a VIRAL Post

When I say "viral", it must be taken into consideration in relatable terms. That means, if a person who has only 500 connections on LinkedIn writes a new post, and it gets 15000 views in the first week, that is a viral post for him. On the other hand, a person with 10k followers writing a post and getting 15k views, would be a "normal post".

This is important to understand because comparing your engagement with someone who has a different size of audience will do you no good.

Case Study: Anshika Gupta

A CS student from a tier 3 college in India gets the opportunity to participate in Amazon wow, an event where she is able to get in touch with the recruiters at Amazon. This led to her coding interview rounds at amazon and she passed them successfully and landed a job at Amazon as an SDE.

She then for the first time writes an emotional post talking about how she didn't clear the exams that "society" thinks are important to be successful in life as an engineer and still made it to a FAANG company, which is rare.

This was her first post on LinkedIn and it literally blew up!

Anshika Gupta · 1st
Incoming SDE at Amazon | Instructor at Coding Elements
1mo · Edited

Woke up this morning and felt like sharing this topsy-turvy ride from Not an IIT/NIT College to Amazon.

.
.
.

I failed in JEE, could not make it to IIT's.
Even, I failed in internships, could not intern at Big Tech.
But Yes, this time I did it.

Life gives you opportunity at every stage, it's just about when you are ready to grab them.

If you are not at your dream place yet, do not think like "Ab kya ab toh final year bhi khatm, jo milna tha mil gaya", or
"IIT toh mila nahi, ab kya karunga", but Work harder, Imprint your goals, and Go achieve them and Make your Reality.

Any tag associated with you could probably define your Past, but neither your Present nor your Future.
#amazon #softwareengineer #think #achieve

This post got around 3 Million views, 100k likes, and 4.3k comments. In other words: CRAZY!

Did she aim to make a viral post? Probably not. And neither should you!

Events like these happen rarely. And so, your goal shouldn't be to make your posts go viral. Your goal should be to make posts each day and try to experiment and see what works for you.

People looking for virality on social media platforms don't understand that it's a long game. There is no short term secret to growth on any social media platform. It's similar to when people buy lottery tickets each year in search of getting rich quickly. And the stats show that 99% of lottery winners end up bankrupt in the next 1 year.

Basically, focus on making posts consistently and learn from what works and what doesn't. There is no magic sauce!

Looking at the post itself, you can see that the post appeals to our emotional senses, which was the main factor that helped it go viral. And this post also had a photo showing her offer from amazon.

Your motive should be to write a post each day, not to go viral at some point, but to get better at your content writing skills.

Another Case Study:

Ishan Sharma
Student @ BITS Goa | Web Developer | ML Enthusiast | Podcast Host | YouTuber...
3d • Edited •

It's funny to see third and final year IIT students flexing their JEE Advanced ranks in their LinkedIn Headlines.

As if they didn't do anything "great" after that entrance exam in their 3-4 years of college life.

What does a great rank in an exam that happened 4 years ago tell you about who they are right now and what they've done?

Makes no sense to me!

#iit #iitjee #college #ishan #accomplishments #achievement #engineering

1,401 • 161 Comments

Reactions

👍 Like   💬 Comment   ↪ Share   ➤ Send

📈 105,537 views of your post in the feed

When writing this post, I never expected it to go viral like it did. I was sharing my thoughts after being on the platform for a year. As you can see, you don't need a lot of hashtags, you only need high engagement.

The sad reality of the social platforms of the present is that controversial pieces of content, content that puts a question on something prevalent in the society, gets higher engagement.

And then people start to miss interpret what the post means and what I wanted to convey. They started a fight on IITs vs BITS based upon what college I am in.

To be honest with you, I have made and shared 10s if not hundreds of posts talking about opportunities, resources, quotes, business related content, and still no one gave that as much attention as they did to this post.

This would be the first post I've written about something controversial and I had no motive of offending people or attacking someone personally.

I learned from this that I could have written it in a better way. But if I did, the post wouldn't have gone so viral. (not that I intentionally wanted it to)

How to get a trending post?

Unlike other platforms, a viral post is not a "trending post" on LinkedIn.

Here are a few of my own trending post notifications.

Congrats, your post has been **trending** in #coding

View hashtag

7h

Congrats, your post has been **trending** in #college

View hashtag

4m

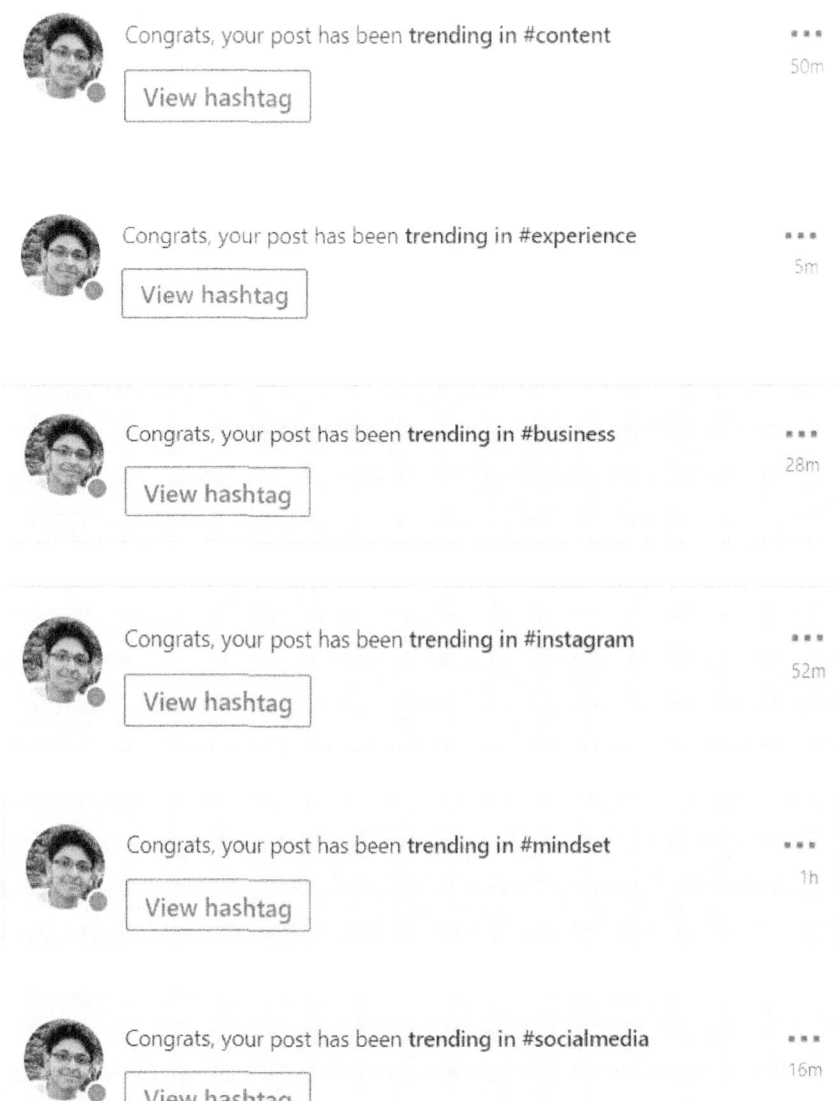

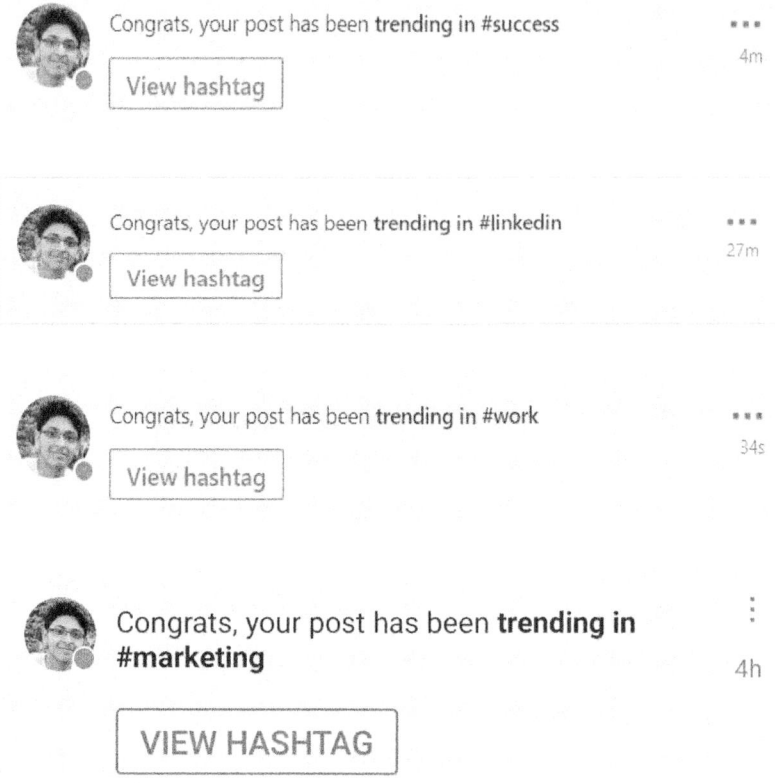

And many more times in the same hashtags!

A trending post appears at the top when you search that hashtag for you. Another interesting thing I observed: these posts of mine, didn't have a lot of engagement or views.

Some people I've talked to say that they look at the percentile of people engaging with the post and not the percentage itself. But it's still a debatable topic. I don't really know how a post becomes trending.

I never thought of making a "viral" or "trending" post idea. I simply create and move on. And so should you! Be in love with the process and not the end product/results.

You can also create polls like this:

This can be a great way to do some market research on any topic and see what the audience really thinks. As you can see, I can understand from this poll that most people read an actual paperback book. And I understand that most people don't consume audiobooks in India.

LinkedIn Video

Sean Cannel, says, "LinkedIn Video might be the biggest opportunity for you in online video going into this new decade (2020 and beyond)."

A couple years ago, LinkedIn added the ability to upload videos. This is HUGE because now you can build a better connection with the person that's viewing your video, than a written word in a text post.

If you wanted to start your YouTube channel, but are afraid that because YouTube is so saturated right now, your content might not be discovered, you can use LinkedIn instead of YouTube.

Right now, you can only upload a video up to 10 minutes but what I've observed is that videos around 2-5 minutes perform really well.

Yes, I understand LinkedIn might not be the alternative for you if you want to make movie reviews or prank videos, but for many people who want to talk about business, entrepreneurship, productivity, their lessons, etc, LinkedIn is a great platform. There are people I'll talk about later in the book who've used LinkedIn video to exponentially increase their followers and reach.

Let's take my own example. I have made many videos for both LinkedIn and YouTube, and I noticed that the same video uploaded on LinkedIn and YouTube had more engagement (views, likes, comments and shares) on LinkedIn than YouTube.

The reason behind this is simple, YouTube has millions of content creators making regular content for years, something LinkedIn doesn't. It's all about demand and supply. YouTube has more supply, hence it's hard for you to compete for attention than LinkedIn, where people are only starting to upload videos.

Now, let's talk about the equipment you need to get started!

Because of the mature audience of the platform, it would be best for you to make a stable video, not a hand held shaking one. You can get started with your phone's back camera.

For audio, you can find very cheap mics to get started with on Amazon and Flipkart. It's recommended that you sound good on a platform like this.

And then the more general advice : make sure you are fully and properly visible and use the golden ratio in your videos.

Christopher Hummel, CEO of FITTEAM does a great job of using LinkedIn video to his advantage. Here's an example of his video posts:

This is what I take away from his strategy here:
1. The video is not more than 1 min.
2. He uses a completion bar to show how much of the video is left.
3. He uses subtitles for people who don't use the speakers or earphones.
4. Video has a square shape with BIG text at top and bottom to grab attention.

5. And he is consistent with it.

There are services like Kapwing that allow you to do just that without knowing anything about how to edit videos.

You don't need to make it look that great when you are starting. Just Start! Quantity will lead to Quality!

There are people like **Goldie Chan** that uploaded one video on LinkedIn each day from 2017 and she made videos for around 700 days straight! She built her following upon the power of video on LinkedIn.

LinkedIn Articles

LinkedIn Articles are your traditional blog - like feature, where you can go in depth on the topic and discuss it properly. There are no known limits to Articles, but I've heard that articles that have more than 120000 characters are not shown by LinkedIn.

Articles give you text formatting features like bold, italics, etc and you can also attach images/gifs in the middle of the article.

Like any other blogs on the internet, making headlines that catch the attention of the person is crucial to its success.

Before you read on : Around October of 2020, LinkedIn's algorithm changed in a way that drastically reduced the organic reach of articles. Like any other platform, LinkedIn keeps messing with what content people see and so you must be able to accept and adapt to these trends.

Writing articles is time consuming, and so I would recommend you to stick to normal status updates which have a limit of 1300 characters. That would be the best for your growth on LinkedIn at the time of writing this book. Although, this might change in a year from now.

Articles allow you to go into depth and establish your authority over that specific niche.

PDF Documents

You can upload Documents that people can view in a post. It looks like an Instagram carousel. And the viewer gets to download it as well.

I've seen startups from my own college like 50xInvestments use documents effectively to their advantage. They make financial reports for various stocks and then share it in a post.

Take a look:

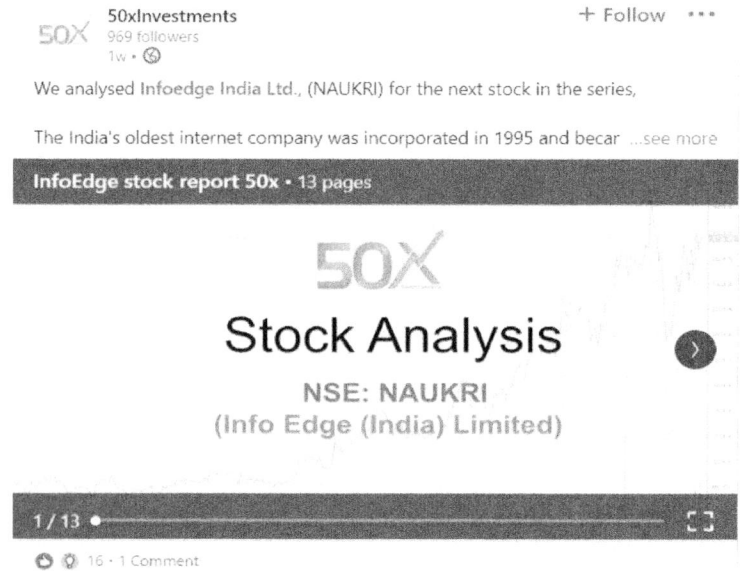

These work great for branding yourself or your business. Just make sure you watermark your PDF document, because there are people who have a tendency to repost without giving credit.

Here's an example of a document I posted some days ago:

There is no limit to the number of slides you can use.

For making these types of PDFs, you can check out Canva. It has helped me out a lot for creating content. Look up on YouTube for how to use it and you'll be good to go!

LinkedIn LIVE

This is a feature that's not available to everyone, and you need to apply to get accepted in it.

Currently, It's used by people to do interviews and do some company announcements. Preksha Kaparwan has really used LinkedIn Live to her advantage. She also uses video to talk about the products and services offered by her company, Alphaa AI.

During her live streams, she and other people from Alphaa AI talk about the features offered by their products and do some QnA as well.

Similarly, If you have your own business and you want to have more brand awareness, consider doing LinkedIn Live each week and see where it takes you.

Doing LIVE interviews is also something I think is interesting and you can try it out as well.

Whenever someone you follow goes Live, you get a notification like this one here:

LinkedIn Profile

Your LinkedIn profile is the virtual representation of yourself. Therefore, you must keep it updated and well maintained.
Here, we'll take a look at the complete profile, it's elements and how to optimize it for search keywords (SEO basically for you digital marketers out there).

Background Image

This is a banner that is present at the top of the profile. Most people make the mistake of not putting anything there. A blank background tells nothing about your personality.

Websites like unsplash, pexels, pixabay, etc come in handy when choosing a background image for your profile.

For example, if you are a developer, you can put an image related to coding.

Tim Ruscica, 320k+ subs YouTuber Founder of Tech with Tim

Rachit Jain, 100k+ subs YouTube

Or if you run a business, then you can put up an image of your business so as to show people what you offer - services or products.

Prudhvi P., CEO @Supervised Learning

BRAND STRATEGIES | INFLUENCER MARKETING | DIGITAL MARKETING

moholla!

www.themoholla.com

Imraan Moh, moholla

Tools like Canva and PicMonkey come in handy when creating banners and graphic design. Or, if you are a graphic designer, feel free to use Photoshop to do this.

People also like to put up photos of their talks that they've been a guest for.

Aishwarya Srinivasan, Data Scientist @IBM Research

These are just a few ideas. Feel free to mix it up and come up with your own background.
The recommended size is 1584 X 396 pixels and you can use a .jpg, .png, or even a GIF file.

Profile Picture

Your profile picture is one of the most important parts of your profile. Most people who are browsing through LinkedIn will see a tiny circle as your profile picture. Hence, its best practice to have a headshot photo with a clear background so that you appear properly even in a tiny circle.

Don't use your photos on the beach or you in a coffee shop sipping coffee. Those might work well for instagram and Facebook, but make sure you stay professional and clean in your profile photo.

If you want to make it look perfect, there is a tool called photofeeler.com where you can put in your photo and people give feedback for your photo on the basis of competency, how likeable you look and how influential it feels.

BUSINESS	20 VOTES
COMPETENT	5.7
LIKABLE	4.6
INFLUENTIAL	5.7

Depending on your profession and your character, you can make sure you find the best photo for your LinkedIn profile.

Make sure your photo is well lit and is a headshot. Feel free to hire a photographer if you can to click a great high definition photo. It'll all be worth it. You have no idea how many people judge you based upon your LinkedIn profile.

Headline

The headline is a one-line statement that gives people a brief idea of who you are.

Why do you need an effective headline? For a couple of reasons:
1. Attract more profile views:
   More profile views lead to LinkedIn suggesting your profile to more people, and so your profile appears more in search. This leads to massive opportunities for you both in job and

There are two two types of Headlines I've seen people make:

Ishan Sharma

Student @ BITS Goa | Web Developer | ML Enthusiast | Podcast Host | YouTuber

This is what most people prefer to use. Using "|" to separate what all you've done.
People also write things like "Ex-Google Ex-Facebook" in their headlines to get more eyeballs on their profiles and it works!

A word of caution: Don't write what you are not. Be honest. I've seen so many people with 10 subscribers, 2 videos and calling themselves a "YouTuber", people writing things like "Entrepreneur" and "Founder". Just make sure you are being true to yourself when writing your headline. It might get you profile views in the short term, but not so much in the long term.

The other type of headline is a sentence, like this:

Rahul Subramanian · 2nd
Here to crack jokes and not to be taken seriously

Sandeep Kochhar · 2nd
Storyteller bleWMinds Consulting. I am a "Failure Ant" that never gives up. 350,000 folks trust me!

These one line sentences arouse curiosity and so people end up viewing your profile and even asking you on a DM, what does that mean? Like this one:

 Ishan Sharma · 7:30 PM
Hey
How do you aim to add 100000 crore into our economy, i'm curious.

Let me know!
Ishan Sharma

So, feel free to think about it and come up with your own.

Here's what you shouldn't write in your headline:

Student at Birla Institute of Technology and Science, Pilani - Goa Campus

I see so many people who write just that. Student at XYZ College. This isn't the most effective headline because this is common and nothing interesting.

When a person is searching for a web developer, he/she would rather click on a profile that has Web Developer written in the headline than your profile that has web developer written in the summary (will be discussed later).

In an ocean of LinkedIn accounts, what makes you different? Think about this and then come up with a headline that would be best for you.

Contact info

Try your best to give them (the viewer or the recruiter) as many ways to contact them as you. If you are a developer or a student, make sure you make your portfolio website and at least host it on GitHub and put its link in the contact info.

I don't recommend giving your phone number though, just because it might not be safe.

If you are active on your twitter account, feel free to mention it in the contact info. And your email should off course be there too. That's 2-3 ways people can contact you.

#OPENTOWORK

The next part you'll see in your profile is a prompt that asks you if you want your profile to be open to get hired. This will only be visible to recruiters looking for hiring people.

For those of you who are already in a job but are looking for job opportunities, you can still turn on the option to show that you are open to work and people from your company will not be able to see that.

In addition to this, there is also an option to add a ribbon on your profile picture that says "OPEN TO WORK" to help you get opportunities faster. You can do that if you do not have a job currently.

About

About is a space to explain who you are, what you do, what you offer, etc.
This is basically your chance to optimize your profile for LinkedIn search.

Write all that you can about you, your previous work experiences, your skills and your hobbies.
Use bullet points and don't make it one giant paragraph, no one has the energy to read it completely.

The mistake many people make here is that they write a couple of lines in the summary and that's it!

This is also not like the Instagram bio caption where you write poetry or some quote. Don't do that. Simply list down your experiences and your skills.

> I am a First year student pursuing Electrical and Electronics Engineering @BITS Pilani Goa Campus. I am always ready to have new experiences, meet new people and learn new things. I find the idea of creating value for people and impacting the world through my work gratifying.
>
> ♦ I am the Podcast Host BITS Cast, a podcast that has been heard over 17000 times by people in 25 countries and Learn To Code w/ Ishan, where I teach people programming languages like Python, Javascript, etc on audio.
>
> ♦ I started a YouTube Channel back in January 2020 which now has more than 1 Lac views and I talk about software development, entrepreneurship, and careers. I have more than a 100 videos uploaded over there.
>
> ♦ I also started a Podcasting service called Pod Infinity in July 2020 where we provide podcast mentor ship and production services.
>
> ♦ I am currently writing a book called "Crush It on LinkedIn" which summarizes my experience of using LinkedIn and it will be a guide for college students to find opportunities, build their brand, and grow their business.
>
> ♦ Also, I am working with multiple businesses to grow their social media platforms and get leads using content. I specialize in creating Carousel decks that convert a stranger to a follower, to a customer.
>
> I am very interested in AI and it's amazing to learn about its applications in various fields like crime detection, predicting diseases like cancer and Parkinson's, use of Big Data to target ads, self driving cars, creation of unique art and music. I am proficient in Python.
>
> I enjoy building projects with Arduino and have been tinkering with electronics since childhood.
>
> ✔ I love video editing and graphic designing and have made more than a 100 videos and carousel decks for LinkedIn and Instagram.
>
> ✔ I enjoy challenges that enable me to grow. I like to find application in what is taught to me and use Feynman and Pomodoro techniques to learn as quickly as possible.
>
> ✔ Having lived all around the country and meeting a lot of people, I'm able to adapt to any surrounding or circumstance.
>
> ★Check out my podcast : https://linktr.ee/bitscast ★

This is what my about section looks like. Detailed, separated with spaces so that it's easier to read and

I've also used certain bullet points and checks that make it more interesting and eye grabbing.

And it also has a call to action at the end, which is a link to my podcast. I encourage you to go look at other people and how they have made their About section and then make your own.

Featured

In the featured section, you can list your major posts, articles, photos, or media links. If you have a YouTube Channel, this is a great place to showcase your channel. If you are an influencer with a public Instagram account, feel free to mention that as well.

You can only list 5 objects that will appear in the featured section. When you add more objects, it adds it into the "See More" option.

Your Dashboard

This section is only visible to you, and it shows statistics of your account. This includes:
1. **Profile Views**
   It simply shows how many people have viewed your profile in the last 90 days. Clicking on it, opens up another page that shows how many people viewed your profile every week in the last 3 months.

   Like this:

   Below that you'll find who these viewers are. If you have a premium account, you'll get to see the profiles of every person who saw yours. If you don't have it enabled, you'll see where the viewers work.
   Here's an example of this:

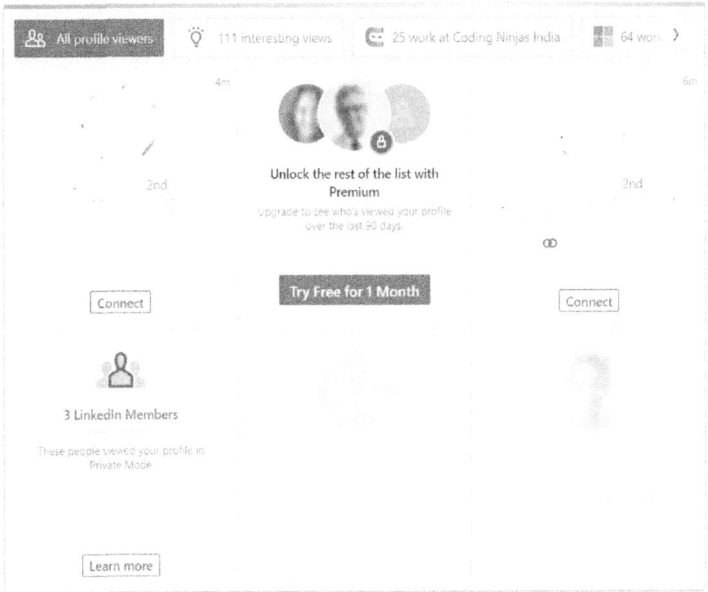

The "Interesting Views" are views from recruiters that are looking to hire people. You can scroll over and it'll show how many people from your college, your club, or other companies viewed your profile.

(I had to censor the names and photos of the people, because I didn't want people messaging me saying I don't want to be featured in a book publicly.)

2. Your Latest Post Views
   This just shows how many people have viewed your latest post or article.

3. Your Search Appearances

Clicking on this option, opens a page that shows how many times your profile appeared using LinkedIn search in the past 7 days, where do the people work at when they found you with search and what their job descriptions are. At the bottom, it also shows what keywords you are ranking for in the search.

```
What your searchers do

Student | 15%
▬▬▬▬▬▬▬▬

Business Strategist | 10%
▬▬▬▬▬

Software Developer | 6%
▬▬▬

Author | 3%
▬

Marketing Specialist | 2%
▪
```

This can be quite insightful when you are optimizing your profile.
Here's an example of what keywords my profile ranks for:

> Keywords your searchers used
>
> Junior Developer
>
> Game Developer
>
> Web Developer
>
> Curator
>
> Python Developer
>
> ⓘ Want to improve future search appearances?

4. Salary Insights
   This opens a page that shows you how much money is earned by people in your field. The stats are based upon what people have reported to LinkedIn. I would say, if you want to get to know how much people are paid in different companies in different locations, go check out glassdoor. It's a website where people give reviews and rating for companies and reveal their salaries as well.
   But in the LinkedIn Salary page, it shows all the positions and how much they are paid, average pay, median pay, and many more details that you can look up.

   You can select the country and what position you are looking for to get more information.

Activity

The activity section shows your latest posts and articles that you've liked, shared or commented on. Clicking on that, opens up your activity dashboard, where you can view your own posts and articles.

Experience

Here's a place for you to list your previous job experiences along with the time duration you worked there for, your job title, and your description. It's really important for you to write what your responsibilities were at that job and what projects you worked on over there. This will give the person looking at the profile a rough idea of your skills, your ability to adapt to new situations and technologies and how much impact you had on the company.

If you are a student working for college clubs, feel free to write what all you did, who projects you worked on, how many sponsors you contacted, how many events you organized, etc. This will help you all the more to get your first internship.

Here's a PRO TIP: Try to get Letters of Recommendation from your previous jobs and attach those for every experience you had.

Also, if you are listing a startup that you did, make sure its LinkedIn Page has a photo, description, etc. That makes it look more REAL.

Education

Simply list down your College/University where you are studying or you graduated from with details like the year of graduation and your stream.

You can mention your 12th grade school and CGPA if you want to, but it's important as far as I know.

Licenses & Certifications

This is the place for you to flaunt your precious certificates that you've earned from online/offline courses or workshops. Feel free to list down what all courses you've done even if it's from sites like Udemy or Lynda.

Also, make sure you link your certificate, so that people can clearly click the link to view the certificate. That's the most transparent way to show that you've ACTUALLY done those courses.

At the end of the day, course certificates might make your profile look legit and amazing, just know that your practical skills and your learnings are worth the most.

Skills & Endorsements

This is the place for you to really display your skills, industry knowledge, tools and technologies and other skills. People who have worked with you can visit your profile and endorse you for those skills. They get the option to tell LinkedIn exactly if they worked with you directly on a project, heard about you from someone, etc.

For example: If you are a developer, feel free to mention all the languages you know, the frameworks, libraries you've worked with, Git and GitHub if you are into open source, etc.

If you want people to endorse you for something, make sure you follow the 1.80$ strategy and take the opportunity to first endorse other people. LinkedIn shows a message to them if someone endorsed a skill and so most of the people end up returning the favor.

You can add up to 44 skills here and this will also help you in optimizing your profile for search.

Accomplishments

The accomplishments section has the following:
1. **Courses**
   You can list all the courses you've attended. If you are in college, you can mention the course names and also basically whichever course you've done that doesn't give you a certificate upfront can be put under this part.

2. **Honors & Awards**

Here, you can mention what all awards and scholarships you've won during college or elsewhere. This is what my Honors and Awards section looks like.

2 Honors & Awards

Intel Edge AI Scholarship
Dec 2019 • Udacity

Learned Implementation of ML Models on Intel's OpenVimo Platform

Udacity Bertelsmann AI Scholarship
Nov 2019 • Udacity

Learned Supervised, Unsupervised Learning Models in Pytorch.

3. **Languages**
This might be helpful if you are doing freelance work for international clients and they might look at it. You can choose your proficiency level for those languages which includes: Native speaker, Professional working proficiency, Elementary, Limited, or Full proficiency.

4. **Projects**
This is one of my favorite parts of the LinkedIn profile. This shows if you are a practitioner of what you show in your certificates you've learned, or just another person on the internet with the fake it till you make it mentality.

What projects have you worked on? What website/apps did you make? Was this a solo project or done in a team?

What were the challenges faced when making this project and how did you overcome them?

Was this a personal project, or a paid for project?

What Software/Technologies were used in it?

Can you show me it's Demo version?

Can I see it's GitHub Repo?[Only for coding projects]

Make sure you answer each of these questions in the description of each project.

If this was done in a group, mention the profiles of those people as contributors.

You can also display the projects you made during Hackathons. Some people are confused with this.

5. **Publication**

    Here you can mention all the times when you were mentioned in a blog post by blogs, or an article you wrote for another blog as a guest writer. Make sure you link the blog/article and give a brief description about it.

6. **Patent**

    This isn't for everyone. It's more specific for researchers and professors. But it's similar to a Publication. In this case, you'll put the link to your patent or research paper.

7. **Organization**
   If you have worked for Non for Profit Organizations, do mention exactly what you did, and how it helped the community overall. For example: You go to teach Village kids a subject like Maths each Sunday. You can mention this saying you taught a 100 village kids Mathematics for X weeks/months.

IMPORTANT

Your normal profile url would be something like this - LinkedIn.com/in/ishan-sharma-12565-234sd
There is an option for you to change that to your own url, like I did - LinkedIn.com/in/ishansharma7390/
This will make it easier for people to discover you by just searching on google your name.

Also, you can generate a CV from your LinkedIn profile using the More option at the top of your profile. But this doesn't look good and you can do a better job with your CV.

LinkedIn recently came up with a CV Builder feature right next to the option to convert profile to PDF, and here you can do some very elementary changes to it. But do check it out once!

Recent Additions

LinkedIn, at the time of writing this, rolled an update that allows you to upload a .mp3 file that would give a pronunciation of your name. This might help when people are looking at people internationally.

Another feature that was rolled out, was double tap to like a photo in a post. This is similar to Instagram and other platforms. It's currently only available on the mobile app though.

Also, you can now show "Support" for the post by tapping the raised hand. Here's what it looks like:

If you don't know, you hover your cursor over the like button on posts to view and choose from these. And you can tap and hold the like button to open this up on the mobile app.

Also, when posting a photo, you can add stickers to it, like these:

And the Stories feature similar to Instagram is also rolling out to more countries. In June, it was released to Australia as the 4th country. People seem to have a love hate relationship with this new feature, but only time will tell if this will go LIVE for everyone.

Testing a new conversational format for LinkedIn: Stories

Published on February 26, 2020

Pete Davies
Consumer Product at LinkedIn. Recovering journalist.

14 articles + Follow

Conversations are at the heart of so much that happens on LinkedIn. Need help with how to manage work life balance? Someone in your community can help share their experience. Have an urgent hiring need — or looking for your next role? Ask your network to make intros. Want to get feedback on your idea? Try messaging or create a post to get opinions from your network.

Last Thoughts

The reality is that anyone on the platform can write whatever they want to. There is no way to verify that that person actually worked at that company. This leads to some people writing and mentioning stuff that they don't know or do.

Also, people are afraid if they put their profile photo, they might get judged by people looking at their profile and could miss an opportunity just because they may not look good to the recruiter.
The only answer that I can give is this: You need to learn to sell yourself, and for that you have to go all in and show yourself online.

People going for software developer interviews think all they need is coding, when in reality, they'll be selling themselves to the company, metaphorically speaking. A person with decent DSA skills and amazing speaking skills will be better than a person with extreme DSA and coding skills who is just not able to properly express themselves.
[Just an example here]

LinkedIn Messaging

One of the most powerful features of LinkedIn is your ability to message people personally.

You have to understand that these are real people and not just a LinkedIn profile. People end up doing self-promotion by sending links to their YouTube channel or asking someone to sign up for some service or like their company page, join a group, etc.

The worst part about it is that they do all this without any context. Without knowing who the person really is.

Some people don't know how to start a conversation and so they never message someone.

This is an example of what I usually do:

Ishan Sharma · 8:47 AM

Hey Evan, I love watching your videos and have learnt a lot from them. Would be great to talk to you on Linkedin

Evan Carmichael · 8:47 AM

Thanks for reaching out Ishan.

We're connected now.

Believe,
Evan

Ishan Sharma · 8:25 PM

So, i see you have successfully cracked GSOC, I will be trying this time in first year. Can you share with me some of the tips for how to choose a particular organization and then go about it?

8:32 PM

Hey,
Refer this: "One stop guide to Google Summer of Code" by Harshit Dwivedi https://link.medium.com/Or3NzJbdx0

Contains all resources and guidance.

Be respectful when asking for help and don't spam someone. People get so many messages each day, it becomes difficult to answer all of them. So, have patience, most people do get back to you in 2-3 days.

Your goal with talking to someone on LinkedIn DMs should be to get them to a video or voice call or even an offline meeting.

You can also make a Group where you would share resources or have discussions on a topic. These can also be engagement groups where people simply put their post links and others open their posts and engage with it early on in order to artificially hijack the engagement rate with your posts.

There's a lot of potential in messaging and you can connect and talk to virtually anyone in the world. Just make sure you are trying to build relationships with people and not trying to sell something to them.

1.80$ Strategy for Growth & Getting Noticed

The best way to grow your LinkedIn account, get more profile views, more connections and opportunities is the 1.80$ Strategy. This was a plan devised by Garyvee back in 2017 and this is what it means.

Firstly, you need to find 10 hashtags that are relevant to your niche. If you are a developer, you can target hashtags like #coidng #developer #programming #softwaredeveloper #softwareengineer #google #microsoft #Facebook #computerscience, etc.

If you want to find out what are the best hashtags for your niche, just search your niche on LinkedIn Search and see what hashtags people are using and figure it out.

Next, everyday you need to search that hashtag on LinkedIn search and look at the top 10 posts and study them deliberately. Feel free to neglect hiring posts if you find those at the top.

Once you have read it completely, comment what you think about it below. And make it meaningful, adding your perspective, your "2 cents".

Do this on the top 9 posts for 10 Hashtags, each day for 3 months, and you'll be surprised to see the response.

This leads to more profile views which helps in search rankings and you'll start to build this personality of a person that has knowledge around that subject matter.

The numbers are arbitrary. You can do more than this, you can do less than this. The point here is to get out there and interact with people in your community.

Now this might seem like a lot of work, and it is to be honest. Reading someone's post and then thinking about it and then putting a meaningful comment is a lot of work. But if it would be easy, everyone would do it. It's hard work, and that's why I know 90% of you reading this won't do it. But the 10% that will, will sweep all its rewards.

Also, this method to grow works for other platforms as well like Instagram and Twitter.

LinkedIn Jobs

Hiring on LinkedIn works in two ways:

1. Either the person reaches out to companies and applies to hiring managers or seeking out for referrals.
2. Hiring managers reach out to you because they found you through your posts or through LinkedIn search.

According to a survey conducted, only 8% of hiring is done by the second method, and most people hustle a lot, sending their resumes with cover letters to 100s of recruiters before hearing anything.

One way is to keep following certain hashtags each day like #hiring #jobseekers, etc. Many recruiters create posts saying that they have all the job openings at their companies and they give you an email to send your CV.

Another method is to check the LinkedIn Jobs Tab where you will find companies posting job openings. You can simply apply to as many as possible and wait for them to reach out to you. This applies both for a full time job and for internships.

You can also search for a specific job role and a location where you can work (remote is also an option) in.

You can also make a post saying that you are looking for work and you have experience in working for X company and you have made these many projects. People will reach out to you in your LinkedIn DMs.

The previous method I talked about for growth also helps out a lot for getting noticed by recruiters.

How Hiring Works

It's very unclear to most people how hiring on LinkedIn works, but I do know that recruiters use LinkedIn heavily to find people for positions. Every company's recruiter gets a premium database service from which they can look for what skills they want to hire for and then move ahead with that.

From what LinkedIn tells us, the LinkedIn search is not the same for everyone. This means, when I type "software developer" in my search, the people that are recommended to me are completely different from what you'll get from your search.

LinkedIn suggests you people that are in your 1st connection circle, then 2nd and so on, it's subjective to everyone of us, sort of like the YouTube homepage.

If you show up higher when someone is searching, you get discovered by more people.

So, how should you rank higher in search results? There are metrics that really matter in determining your rank, these are : Profile views and Keywords.

Profile Views

Similar to any other social media, profile views are basically the number of times people visit your profile, in a given time frame. When a profile has more views, LinkedIn understands that the person is more famous and so, it pushes the profile higher in search results.

Keywords
Your headline, the text right below your name plays a major role in telling LinkedIn who you are and what category you belong to. Your profile summary + skills along with the headline affect what keywords are you optimised for (More on optimising your profile in the later chapters).

A survey conducted by Andrew LaCivita (who runs a YouTube channel on career advice), shows that 8% of people that are hired in companies said, "someone on LinkedIn contacted them about it".

You'll find a section right below your headline, that asks if you're looking for a job. You can turn it on, and it will only be visible to the recruiters that are looking to hire people. Make sure you select what positions you are suitable for and what locations, you can join the office.

LinkedIn Advertising

Advertisements on LinkedIn appear in multiple places. Here are some examples:

This one is a simple ad to learn more about their services.

GlobalWebIndex
17,746 followers
Promoted

That's the percentage of people who say they watch TV and use a device at the same time. Discover more insights like this in our global entertainment r ...see more

Entertainment Trends Around the World Report
globalwebindex.com

Download

This one offers a report/ebook as a lead magnet to grow their email list and spread brand awareness. This does take a lot of time to make but in the end, you do get a ton of emails too if targeted properly.

Sendbird
4,241 followers
Promoted

Learn how to focus on problems to solve rather than features to ship during our Q&A webinar with Bruce McCarthy, founder of Product Culture.

LIVE WEBINAR
Product roadmaps relaunched

Bruce McCarthy
Product Manager of Product Culture

July 16, 10am PST, 1pm EST

Register now

sendbird

Register for the Product Roadmaps Relaunched Webinar
get.sendbird.com

Register

This one is another way to grow your email list but with the help of a live webinar on some topic. This might take less effort initially but people might not opt in due to busy schedules.

Ad

DMI Finance is a tech-driven, new-thinking provider of credit solution

DMI FINANCE

Technology - Innovation - Partnership

Follow

This type of ad appears on the right side of your feed and can be to follow the page or check out their jobs listings.

B2B Digital & IT Services - Hundreds of Agencies at your fingertips. Save Time & Money on your Projects Ad

This is a banner ad that you can see at the top of your profile.

I have used the ads manager on LinkedIn with the initial Rs. 2500 free Ad credit that I got to run an ad. The problem here is that the CPC can be quite high when compared to Facebook and Instagram. On the other hand, you do get a more professional crowd on LinkedIn.

And if you've ever worked with Facebook's Ad Manager, you'll find this to be quite similar. You can do the same type of detailed targeting like you can do on Facebook and select where you want your ads to appear.

If your business offers B2B solutions, LinkedIn advertising might work out for you.

For most other businesses, I would recommend them to just create organic content just because of the free reach right now.

Yes, you'll have to make multiple pieces of content but it will be so worth it.

I won't go into detail talking about Detailed targeting and making campaigns, that would be a whole another book. You can look it up on YouTube or get some courses on sites like Udemy and get started.

Don'ts on LinkedIn

Here, I share some examples of malpractices people do on LinkedIn which are depricative for your rapport and your profile.

Sending improper messages in DM

Computer Engineer

TODAY

 James 7:20 pm
So sorry to infringe on your privacy,your profile seems really nice you're beautiful, i would like to know you better and be a friend or more

This is a message one of my connections got in her DMs and it really annoyed her!

By now, I hope it's clear to you, that LinkedIn is a professional platform, and you really should consider other casual platforms for conversations like these.

Use of Cursing/Slang or Hate Speech

Even Gary Vaynerchuk decided to beep out the cursing in the videos he puts out on the platform. Use it to grow yourself and others, and not to tear someone apart. LinkedIn is far from Facebook and hate speech will not be tolerated in this community. This might seem obvious to many, but I just wanted to point this out.

Writing the Profile Summary in Third Person

I see many people using third person to describe who they are in the summary, and that's just not correct. If you think about it, your profile is your digital presence on the platform and you must always describe yourself in first person form.

Plagiarised Content

I see this happen a lot and even Imraan Moh(Founder of Moholla, a digital marketing agency) talked about this on my podcast. Often, it happens that a person with a large following looks at another person's post and they end up copying it.

It happened to me too. I had a post with a picture talking about my best reads of 2019, and someone else copied that image for his own post and claiming it as his own.
If you really want to use someone else's content, simply give credits in your post or article, it's great for both you, and the person who's content you're using

Spamming People in LinkedIn DMs

Don't do this. I see a lot of people just randomly messaging me to join their group, to subscribe to their channel, sign up for their events, etc.
Remember, DMs is for building a connection with a person and trying to solve their problems, not yours. Try to strike up a conversation first, provide some context before pitching them your product. Try to get them on audio/video calls to tell about yourself.

I like what Mr. Kennedy said, "Ask not what the country can do for you, ask what you can do for your country". In this case, the country is the person on the other side, your 'could be' customer.

Not Connecting to Everyone on LinkedIn

Many of my friends think that they should only connect with people they know on the platform, not with everyone on the platform, as a result most of their connections are from the same college.

I say you should absolutely connect with everyone in your 'niche'. For example, if you are a college student into software development, connect with people like you, studying in any college around the world that are also interested in software development.

Especially, if you are looking for jobs, you should try as often as possible to connect to people that are already working in those roles, and even interact with them. You will be surprised to see how many people would like to talk to you about it. You can also leverage them by asking for referrals once you've established a connection with them, which would be beneficial for both of you.

[Many companies have a referral program, where an employee can refer a person to be hired. And if the person get hired, the employee get a bonus, so it becomes a win win situation for both]

The bigger your connection circle is, the more opportunities you'll get.

Success Story of Lewis Howes

Lewis Howes is a former professional football player, world record holding athlete turned lifestyle entrepreneur. He is the podcast host of the famous School of Greatness podcast.

But he wasn't like this from the beginning. Infact, he had a point in his life when he was jobless, unmotivated and had spent his days sitting at a couch watching television in his sister's house. It was a career ending injury that put his life on halt back in 2007.

Then, one day, his friend calls him telling him to join LinkedIn [which was ancient in it's functionality back in 2007]. It's an online community of business professionals having expertise in their subject of matter.

Lewis put all of his concentration into learning about the technicalities of LinkedIn and spent every single hour of his day, interacting with people on the platform.

After realising the problems people face in connecting with other sports professionals, he went on to make a LinkedIn group called 'Sports Industry Network'. In only a year, the group reached 10,000 members. He continued creating more city specific groups on LinkedIn.

He was enabling people to get to new opportunities in the group. People started thanking him for it and he started growing his network this way.

He started organizing meetups for free initially to meet people in his groups and establish a deeper connection.
Later on, he met Joel Comm, author of the best selling book 'The Adsense Code : What google never told you about making money with adsense' and made him realize the power of LinkedIn for business owners. Joel added Lewis to his panel of experts who use to run webinars for business owners.

Lewis found his passion in teaching people the power of LinkedIn and ended up making "big money" in that first webinar alone. This gave Lewis the confidence to continue doing these webinars.

He then leveraged his LinkedIn network to talk to influential people in various fields on an interview type podcast that is now known as "School of Greatness".

None of this could've been possible without LinkedIn. He wouldn't have met so many people without taking the first step in learning how the platform works.

Coming Soon: LinkedIn Stories

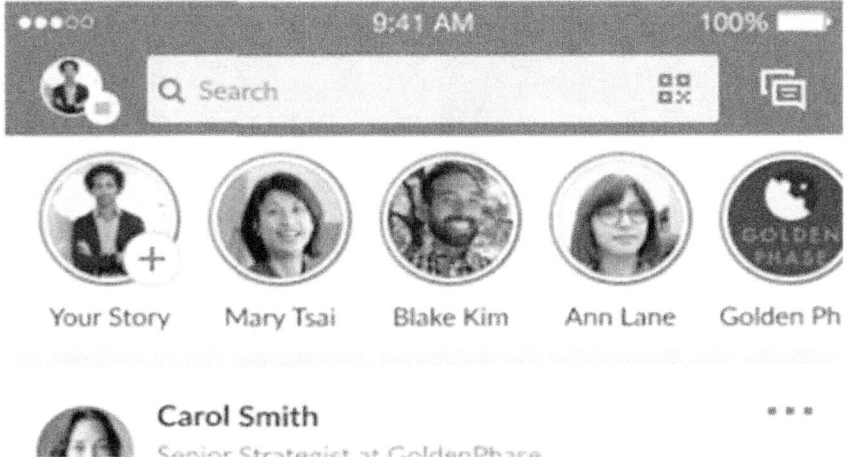

  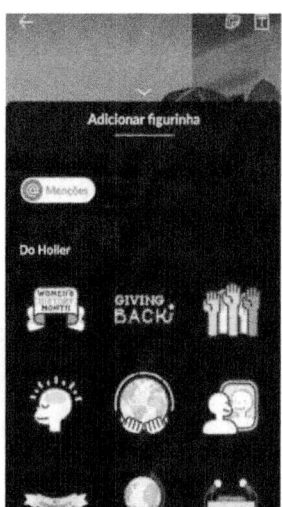

At the time of writing this book, LinkedIn just announced that they'll be adding a new feature called "Stories", similar to Instagram, Snapchat and other platforms you may be familiar with.
This is a BIG deal, as stories will lead to people sharing more parts or their lives with their connections on LinkedIn. This also tells us that Microsoft is taking LinkedIn to a platform more like Facebook, but for professionals.

The update will probably be released worldwide by the end of this year, and it'll be exciting to see how people use their creativity for using stories.

Similar to Instagram, whenever LinkedIn pushes out a new feature like stories, it promotes people that use this feature, as an appraisal system. This I believe is another great opportunity for you to get discovered by more people on LinkedIn.

I have seen multiple posts on LinkedIn by people who are using it say that it will ruin the platform which was made especially for professionals.

But let's not go into that before using it first.

As you can see in the images, you can write something, add stickers and even tag people in there. You also get the option to choose who all can view it.

The rest of the mechanism is very much the same way Instagram and Snapchat operate on.

Use it or Lose it!

So, I've tried to explain to you the benefits of using LinkedIn to show people who you are and what you do. Opportunities like these only come once in a decade, last decade it was YouTube and now you know how difficult it is for a person to get attention (it's relatively hard, in case you don't know).

You must act NOW, and start optimizing your profile with keywords, produce content, and building relationships with people on LinkedIn. Again, one of the most important factors for your growth on any platform is your Frequency and Consistency.

There are thousands of people using LinkedIn to create their influence, or get hired or expand their businesses, and I hope the same for you! This will only get harder as years pass by, and so you must start utilising this opportunity TODAY!

I saw a post recently on grabbing opportunities by Salil Naik that really hit home for me.

> **Salil Naik** · 1st
> Award-Winning Developer | Putting Goa on the world's tech map
> 15h ·
>
> Many people ask me how I get so many #opportunities while still being a student and my answer remains the same. I take the opportunities that you leave.
>
> People lose most of the opportunities because of their habit of rejecting themselves. You might have noticed this trend. The ones who are active, strive to be proactive and the ones who are passive, always remain passive. Some students will have many projects and awards to their names while others will have nothing to brag about.
>
> Is it because there are fewer opportunities? No. It's because we don't realize that to get the opportunities, we need to take the opportunities.
>
> Let me give you an example; There is a lot of profit in selling cars. Taking a dealership of any big brand is gonna make you a fortune; but to take that dealership, you have to invest heavily. That's the reason the rich get richer and the poor get poorer. And this gap will always be there.
>
> The same goes for opportunities. The one who grabs every opportunity that comes his way will get to know about more opportunities. And you cannot grab an opportunity unless you know about it. So stop doubting your worth, stop rejecting yourself, and take the very next opportunity that comes your way. And believe me, it will open a world of opportunities for you. #hustle
>
> 👍❤️💡 39 · 3 Comments

Looking at the statistics, I know that many of you were affected due to the pandemic/lockdown, some even lost their jobs, or their offers were canceled, or experienced pay cuts. In these hard times, using LinkedIn can be so helpful to find new opportunities and build new relationships.

At last, I would like to remind you that the end goal of using LinkedIn is to create a connection with people, and bring them out into the world.
You've read it all, now GO EXECUTE!

Printed in Great Britain
by Amazon